Park Songs

a poem/play

David Budbill (signature)

Photos by

R. C. Irwin (signature)

Exterminating Angel Press

Portions of this book first appeared, some in different form, on the
Exterminating Angel Press online magazine at *www.exterminatingangel*.com

EXTERMINATING ANGEL PRESS
"Creative Solutions for Practical Idealists"
Visit *www.exterminatingangel.com* to join the conversation
info@exterminatingangel.com

Exterminating Angel Press book design by Mike Madrid
Typesetting by John Sutherland

ISBN 978-1-935259-16-9
eBook 978-1-935259-17-6
Library of Congress Control Number: 2012935086

Printed in The United States of America

Distributed by Consortium Book Sales & Distribution
(800) 283-3572 www.cbsd.com

Park Songs

There was never yet an uninteresting life. Such a thing is an impossibility. Inside the dullest exterior there is a drama, a comedy, and a tragedy.
—**Mark Twain**

Numberless are the world's wonders, and none more wonderful than man.
—**Sophocles**, *Antigone*

We learn in a time of pestilence that there is more to admire in men than to despise.
—**Albert Camus**, *The Plague*

for Nadine and Mia
may you persevere and prosper

The People of the Park
(In Order of Appearance)

Mr. C.—Would-be poet, keeper, attendant and guardian of the Park.

Various homeless people who sleep in the Park.

Haal—Hangs Around A Lot.

The Purse Lady—Always well and formally dressed. She carries a black patent leather purse.

Kathy—A more or less homeless teenaged girl. Daughter to Nancy.

Shaun—A young man with Tourette's Syndrome.

Judy—Partner to Nancy. Caretaker to Wayne.

Nancy—Partner to Judy, mother to Kathy.

Wayne—Judy is his caretaker.

Sue—Mother to Jesse.

Jimmy—A widower.

Fred—Fancies himself a lady's man.

Jeanie—A waitress.

Jesse—Son to Sue.

Mary—A maid in a motel

Isaiah—A street preacher.

Miss Forty—Maybe an outpatient from a local mental institution, maybe not.

Various other unidentified people in the Park at various times.

The action of PARK SONGS takes place during a single day.

Part One

RISE AND SHINE

Early morning, the Park, Mr.C. enters.

Rise and shine. Rise and shine. Rise and shine, my pretties.
Who wants to work today? Does anybody want to work today?
I got to get you out of here, folks. My daylight clientele returneth.
Who wants to work today? It's twenty-five dollars
for eight short hours--cash at the end of the day.

What's the job?

This work order says: put the rubber bands and little red straws
on cans of WD-40 for eight short hours and you got twenty-five
big dollars. Come on, Ladies and Gentlemen, you know you've got
to have it. Some pay today means a bottle to sleep with tonight.
Twenty-five dollars today means sweet oblivion tonight.
Rise and shine, my pretties. Rise and shine!

You gonna work today?

Nah.

Come on, you better work today.

Nah.

Where you gonna go?

I don't know. I'll find someplace.

Come on, folks. It's either hi ho hi ho it's off to work you go

or you godda get out of the Park 'til ten o'clock tonight.
You all know the drill.

Rise and shine. Rise and shine.

HAAL

Hi, Mr. C. Hi. Good morning.

Hello, Haal. Beautiful morning, isn't it? Beautiful day.

It sure is, Mr. C. It's a beautiful day. And I've got a beautiful feelin' ...

I know the rest, Haal.

Oh, croix-sant! croix-sants is my favorite. Thanks a lot Mr. C. You're a pal. You're a pal to Haal, Mr. C.

Yeah. Yeah.

Got any new pomes today?

Yeah. I got a new one.

Well . . . can I hear it?

Sure. It's called "Yesterday on My Way Home from the Store."

Oh, that's a good title, Mr. C. That's a real real good title, Mr. C.

You want to hear it or not?

Well, of course I do. Don't get mad at me, Mr. C. Sure I do. I want to hear it. Sure.

Then let me read it.

Okay.

Okay. "Yesterday on My Way Home from the Store"

**I saw a huge Black man   in an overcoat   on a street corner
his back to the street   facing a vacant lot   in which there was
a pile of bricks and plaster and dirt and cement   and this huge
Black man   was staggering,   swaying,   back and forth,
and his knees buckled from time to time,   and   he was
standing,   you might say,   moving in place   as if he were
marking time   to a tune with a   bizarre tempo,   a tune
someone else   was forcing him   to march to,   and   this
huge Black man who was   staggering, swaying,   standing,
you might say,   marking time   to somebody   else's tune,
was flailing his arms about in front of himself   and throwing
punches   at that pile of rubble   or at someone   in front
of himself   who wasn't there, and   this huge Black man
(I know this)   smelled   like alcohol   and piss.**

**Yesterday   on my way home from the store   I saw a huge
Black man   and   he was shouting   and crying.
He was crying.**

That's a nice one, Mr. C. Pretty.

Pretty?

Yeah, I thought it was pretty.

**Yeah, well, a lot of good it'll do me. Say, listen, it's time for me
to go to the P.O., pick up the mail, see which set of literary
snoots, snots and assholes rejected me today.
Guard the fort here for a little while, will ya, Haal?**

I sure will, Mr. C. I'll watch things. Nothin' gonna get away from me.

HAAL AND THE PURSE LADY

That's my friend. That's Mr. C.
He's my pal. He's a pal to Haal.
We have breakfast here together
every day.

Huh.

He's a poet. He writes poetry.

I know that.

He's gone down to the Post Office
to see who rejected him today.

Huh.

He's comin' back.
Here he comes right now.

YOU SHOULD PUT LIGHTS: THE PURSE LADY AND MR. C.

You work here?

Yes, I work here.

You should put lights up here. You ever been here after dark?

You know I have.

Around dark? I mean when it gets dark? It's not safe.
Not anymore. Not like it used to be. It's too dark at night. And it's
an eye-sore. You should clean up this place. You should put lights.
I mean, it's not right: this place. You work here?

Yes. I work here.

It used to be so nice, very nice, so beautiful. A Japanese garden.
And taken care of. You just don't know. Why, when your mother
was alive . . . . I knew your mother. I knew her. . . .

Ma?

Your mother.

You did not. I keep telling you, you never knew her.
How many times I got to tell you? You never knew her.

She gave us this park. She told me I could sit here anytime,
anytime I wanted.

She did not.

And I did too. I still do. I've got the permission.

You don't got the permission.

But it's not the same. Not anymore. You work here?

Yes! I keep telling you.

It's not right the way it is now. It's too dark at night and, well, look at it. It's not right. You should put lights. This neighborhood's not the way it used to be. Not anymore. I've lived here all my life.

You have not.

Of course, I don't mean here. Not right here. I'm not like them. I have an apartment, a very nice one too--if I do say so myself-- just a couple blocks from here. I've been there forty years.

You have not.

Forty years. But it's not like it used to be, I mean this place. Huh. I guess not. My apartment is, because I take care of it. It's neat and clean. Not like this place. Just look at it. It's awful now. It's a parking lot.

I know.

A human being parking lot. And it's too dark at night. You should work here.

I do work here!

You should put lights.

KATHY AND SHAUN

Hi Shaun.

**Hi Kathy. Hi Kathy. Nice hair, nice hair. Nice hair, Kathy.
YO! BABE! Nice hair.**

Boy, you're here early today.

**Yeah. Had to get out of the house. Had to get away. YEOW!
I took the 104. I take the 104 down here. I know the driver.
He knows me. He's not afraid of me. I think . . . I think he
even kinda likes me. I hope he likes me. I think he does.
I think he kinda looks forward to seeing me every day. OW!
He knows, he knows me, you know? We like to talk to each
other. That's why, that's why, that's why, YEOW!
That's why I take the 104.**

You take the 104?

**Sure. Sure. Sure. Even though, you know, I got
to walk ten blocks out of my way to catch it.**

You take the 104 to here?

**Yeah. I got energy. I got lots YO BABE! of energy. He likes me.
The driver of the 104, I mean. We like each other. Like us,
I mean. Like we YEOW! do. Like we like each other. I mean, like,
I like the 104, like I like it here, like I like you, Kathy.
HEY! YEOW! You know?**

JUDY AND NANCY

I can't talk anymore. I got to go.
I've got to see what Wayne can do today. I love you.

Don't say it if you don't mean it.

I know we're not finished with this, I know we're not, but what you need to know is: I love you.

Okay. Okay.

I do.

Okay!

You do this. You always do this.

Do what?

What you did.

Did I say I didn't believe you? I heard what you said.

Why are you always so angry!

I'm not.

You're not angry?

I'm not always so angry. But you're always so cool. You're always so goddamned cool! It's like you're always a million miles away.

I just disappoint you all the time. Nancy, this has got to stop.

Fine.

I've got to go.

Fine.

See? You did it again.

Did what?

That.

What?

That.

That?

That! What you always do. Nancy, I've got to go to work.
Listen, no matter what you say, I am here for you.
You can count on me.

I can count on you?

Yes.

Count? Well, as I've said before, it doesn't add up to much.

Don't start that again! We can't go through all that again!
I've got to go to work!

Fine. Good-bye.

Oh, God! I wish you wouldn't do that!

Do what?

No! I won't! I'm not going over it again!

Fine. Good-bye.

JUDY AND WAYNE: I CAN'T DECIDE

Okay. You go ahead and see how you do. You can do it.

Do what?

Take a little walk by yourself, Wayne, just like we talked about.

I don't think so.

Don't start that again. We can't go through all that again.
If you need me, come and get me.

I don't think so.

Wayne, come on. I'll be right here
and then after you get going I'll follow you.

I don't think so.

You can do it.

I don't think so.

Yes you can. Try it.

I can't decide.

You can do it.

**No. No. I can't decide. I can't decide!
I can't do it! I can't decide.**

Try it again. Try it. Try.

He tries again. Hesitates. Then timidly steps off on a path.
When he reaches the other side of the Park he turns and
looks at Judy, raises his fist and says:

Yes!

SUE AND NANCY

Hi, Nancy.

Hi, Suzie.

What are you doing here at this time of the day?

I go in late today.

You don't sound too good.

**I'm not. I don't know, Suzie, I just can't stand it anymore.
I don't know what I'm going to do. Every time I take a deep
breath and let down my guard for even just a second, I get
blindsided by something else.**

**Kathy took off a couple of weeks ago and I'm pretty sure
she stole some money I had stashed away. I can't prove it
because I can't remember exactly how much was there,
but I've got my suspicions. On the other hand I was so glad
to have her gone, to be rid of the way she tortured me,
that I'm not really all that sorry to lose the money.**

Kids.

Yeah. You?

Same. Jesse's driving me up the wall. He's at me all the time.
And the older he gets the worse he gets.

And it'll just get worse and worse.

Great.

I'm sorry. I don't mean to make it worse than it already is. I wish I could make it better.

I wish you could too. Why does it have to be this way?

I'm not the one to ask.

My mother could of helped me now. And maybe if Jesse'd known her, maybe if we could have been more of a family than just, ya know, him and me, maybe he wouldn't be the way he is now. I don't know. I don't know what I'm going to do.

I don't either. . . for you or for me. Jesus! We make a great pair.

Yeah, well, misery does love company.

I guess it does.

I got to go. I'm gonna be late. I'm on my way to get Jesse. I promised him I'd take him to get an iPhone.

Mind if I walk along with you?

That'd be nice.

MR C. AND POETRY, ONCE

*Mr. C enters the Park. He paces back and forth
talking to someone who isn't there.*

Wait a minute! Wait a minute, you Bastard!
You can't talk to me that way! Who do you think you are!
I was reading all those names you're always dropping
before you could read! Don't condescend to me you provincial,
tin-eared ambitionist. Just because Don Pullen plays the piano
with his forearms and his fists does not mean he can't play Rachmaninoff;
it means only he chooses not to! If I choose to speak
in an archaic tone; salubrious and beautiful, cadenced and
melodious, I can! Which is to say: I actually, premeditatedly,
deliberately and consciously speak in this harsher tongue, in
vulgar tones, mordant, acrimonious, base,
insulting, pedestrian and contemptible, because
in this gross speech, I hear a lyric beauty--the untutored
crassness, the common moans--that overflows my soul and I
know a sense of love and oneness with ordinary people which
lifts me up above the arrogant literati, like you, you little twerp,
and I float on these common songs to a place I know as home
which sure as hell ain't where you come from
you narrow-minded little asshole.

All of which is, in short, to say: you should not mistake my
modesty for stupidity, I certainly do not mistake your arrogance
for intelligence!

JIMMY AND FRED

Jimmy!

Hi, Fred.

Well I'll be . . . It's nice to see you out here in the air.
I've missed you.

Nice to see you too.

Are you holding up?

**I'm tryin' to. But it's not easy. I'm depressed, Fred.
I don't want to do nuthin'.**

Are you getting out?

**Not much. Once in awhile, but not too much. It's hard, Fred.
I got to kick my ass out the door. I want to stay at home,
sit in my chair and stare at the wall. I don't want to come
out here.**

I'm sorry Jimmy. I wish that there was something I could do.

I wish that there was something you could do too.

I live alone too, you know. It's not the same for me, I know, but . . .

I appreciate your sympathy, but it don't help much.

I'm sure it doesn't.

I don't want to be here.

It's good for you.

That's what everybody says.

It's true.

I don't see why it is. Why is it?

You'll waste away if you don't. You got to go on with your life.

What if I don't want to! What life have I got left?
Aw, I don't mean to take it out on you, Fred.
But every morning when I wake up, I'm sorry I didn't die.
I hate life, Fred.

Are you going out with any women?

Aw, I did once or twice. It's no good. It makes it worse.
Gold diggers. All of 'em. They're all out to hustle a buck
until they find out I don't have one.

Yeah.

Besides, they're all too set in their ways.

Don't I know.

Not that I ain't. I know I am and I like it that way too.
I don't want to change. And they don't want to either.
So what's the use? It's hard, Fred.

I'm sorry, Jimmy.

Thanks. I know you are. I'm sorry too.

I got to get my lunch. I'm glad to see you out here, Jimmy.
It's nice to see you out here. Hang on, Jimmy.

Why?

Say, I'm going over to the Diner. Why don't you come with me.
Let's go see what kind of soup they got today.

I'm not very much for company.

I noticed that.

But it would be nice.

Good.

**You know, Helen and I, we used to like to go to the Diner.
We used to go there twice a week. We'd go for lunch and then
we'd come out here and sit in the Park and take the sun.**

Why don't we have our lunch and then you and I go fishin'.
You ain't been down to the lake since I can't remember when.
Some of the boys been catchin' some big cats, Jimmy, big cats.

Well, I don't know. Let's have our lunch and then we'll see.

Fair enough.

Does that waitress . . . what was her name?

Jeanie.

Yeah, Jeanie. Does Jeanie still work there?

She still does.

Now there's a cute one for ya. I tell you, I'd like to cuddle up with that one. If it was forty years ago, I'd make a play for that one.

Hi, Suzie. Sorry I'm late.

Not very.

What do you mean?

What do you mean what do I mean?

You don't have to get so testy.

I'm not.

You are! I mean, really, I'm sorry I'm late. It's no big deal.

I know it's not. I know you are.

Then how come you were so sarcastic?

I was?

You said "not very."

I know.

Well, I tried hard to get here when we said.

Oh, no, I meant not very late.

Oh, I thought you meant not very sorry.

No.

Oh.

I'm sorry.

Me too.

We're both sorry. So anyway, what's new with you?

Ah, I don't know. Nothing. That's the trouble. Nothing's ever new. I'm 27 years old and I feel like my life is over. Am I going to spend the rest of my life waiting tables at the Diner?

The Diner is nice and all that and it's not a bad place to work, the pay's okay and the tips are pretty good--a lot better than when I waited table at that veggie-reggie-hippie-dippy restaurant. Kripes, all those left-wing, power-to-the-people types are the tightest fisted, holier-than-thou crabs I ever met.

The Diner isn't like that. The folks are friendly and the tips are good.

Really?

Yeah. It's not all up here with them, in the head I mean. The ones who come into the Diner aren't that way. For them it's in the stomach, where it counts. If they got money, they share it.

I like it there. I do. But . . . I mean . . . it's a diner! How am I gonna meet a guy in a place like that?

What's so great about a guy?

You're so bitter, Suzie. It doesn't have to always turn out like it did for you.

That's what you think.

Yeah, that is what I think. The guys who come into the Diner are pretty nice, most of 'em . . . some of 'em . . . well . . . . I just want a chance.

I don't know. I'm in a rut. I get off work. I got all that grease and cigarette smoke in my hair and uniform . . . I hate that.

So I go home. I take a shower, wash my hair and I put on some clean clothes. I feel better. I feel good. I smell good. I like myself that way, all clean and sweet and smelling good.

So what do I do? I go down stairs and I have dinner with Mom. And then the rest of the evening I watch TV . . . with Mom.

I mean, Suzie, I'm 27 years old and I'm workin' in a diner and I'm still livin' at home . . . with Mom! She's in my life, everywhere in my life! Every time I step out the door, when it's not to work, I mean, she's at me with all kinds of questions . . . It's like I'm 12 years old; like I'm in jail!

Why don't you get your own place?

I don't know. I guess I should.

Maybe if you two could live apart you could get along.

I doubt it. Besides, what would she do without me? She can't get along without me. She'd fall apart without me.

Maybe not. Maybe if the two of you could live apart you wouldn't be at each other's throats all the time.

I can't imagine that. I'm sorry but I can't.

Is this all there is, Suzie? The Diner every day, come home, a shower, then dinner and TV with Mom? Is that all there is? What am I going to do?

I'm sorry, Jeanie.

Look at it this way if you want; at least you got a Mom. My mother died when I was 19. Jessie never knew her. When I talk to him about her, he doesn't even know who I mean.

I had so many things I wanted to talk to her about, things about my childhood, questions to ask her, things we never talked about while I was growing up. But she died before I got the chance to do that. It's a dirty trick.

I wanted to ask her if she'd ever had an affair.

Could you have?

Yeah, I think so. You know, just honest, no how-could-you . . . . The two of us with each other, close to each other, maybe we're holding hands, and at the same time both of us sort of watching, looking at what had happened, both of us, you know, amazed at what happens . . . .

We all ought to have that chance at least once in our lives. Shouldn't we? I feel cheated. I wanted to be with my Mom. I want to be with her. I want to be with my Mother!

I got to get back to work.

I'll walk you back.

NANCY AND KATHY

How long have you been back?

About a week.

What have you been doing?

Hangin' out.

You got money?

Some. . . . Don't ask me where I got it.

I didn't plan to.

Good.

You're not coming back.

Did I say I wanted to?

It's too late.

Did I say anything?

I won't do it.

I didn't say anything!

JUDY AND WAYNE: I'M WORRIED

Okay now. This time I want you just to walk from here
to that bench over there and sit down and stay there. I'll go away
just for a few minutes and then I'll come back and get you.

I don't think so.

Come on now, don't start that again. You can do this.
Just remember what you did before. That was a lot harder than this.
You walked all the way through the park and went out on
the other side, and who was with you?

Nobody.

Exactly. You did such a great job on that one and all by yourself.
You can do a great job on this one too. I know you can. Okay?
Are you ready?

Yeah.

Good. Now you just sit there, and I'll be back in just a few minutes.

**I'm worried. I'm worried about my stomach. I've got these pains
in my stomach, and then up a little . . . up a lot. It's there
all the time. It never goes away. I mean the pain. And
it moves around sometimes. It moves around a lot. Over here
to my left side and then across and over to my right side,
and sometimes it's in my back--I mean the pain . . . up and
down my spine and on my sides. Once in a while . . . sometimes
. . . a lot . . . it shoots down my leg about half way to my knee,
all the way to my knee, down to my ankle. My ankle hurts
all the time. The pain is there all the time. It never goes away.
I'm worried. I'm worried about my stomach, and I'm worried
about my foot. I've got a pain in my foot. My left foot and only**

on the left side of my left foot, the left half of my left foot. Isn't that strange? What causes that? I've been to the doctors and they say there's nothing there. Well! I can feel there's something there--in my stomach, in my foot. I've got these pains in my stomach, in my back, in my leg, and in my foot and I can't sleep. I get so worried I can't sleep. Sometimes I go days and days without any sleep. What causes that? I wonder what causes that. I'm worried about my stomach and my foot and about why I can't sleep. And I'm worried about I might go crazy. What if I go crazy?

How did it go?

Let's go back now. I want to go back now.
Let's go back now. I want to go back now.

THE iPHONE

No, Goddamnit, Jesse, no. I said no.

But you promised I could have an iPhone!

I don't care what I said. The answer's no.

You promised!

It's too expensive!

You promised!

Stop whining, Jesse!

You liar! You goddamned liar!

Your mouth! Stop it. I mean it.
If you don't stop . . .

Liar! Goddamned liar!

THE LIFE HURTS BLUES

This life hurts.
    It's full of misery and pain.
One long sorrow song,
    and every day's the same.

I wish I wasn't livin',
    wish I didn't have a name,
wish I'd never known my Mama,
    and I wish my Daddy never came.

This life hurts.
    It's full of misery and pain.
One long sorrow song,
    and every day's the same.

One long sorrow song,
    and every day's the same.
How I wish I, how I wish I
    did not have a name.

KATHY, JESSE, AND SHAUN

Hey, Jesse.

How'd you know my name?

Your Mom was screamin' it, remember?

I remember.

I'm Kathy. You want to hang with us?

I guess.

Jesse this is Shaun. Shaun this is Jesse.

> Hey Jesse. Jesse Hey. Jesse Jesse Hey.
> Jesse Hey. Jesse Hey. Jesse Jesse Hey.

He's okay.

> Yeah, I been comin' here a long time. A long time.
> OW! It's a neurological disorder, ya know? It's called
> Tourette's Sydrome. Ya know? Ya know? HEY OW!
> I used to get a little OW! OW! Social Security check,
> a small one, but OW! HEY OW! it got canceled. Ya know?

Can't you take some medicine?

> Well you can, I can, I do, I did, I have, and it takes care of
> some of the symptoms some of the time, some of the
> time, sometimes, but then side FUCK YOU! YOU BASTARD!
> effects and other things get worse than what you had
> before, for me, I mean, I mean, I mean for me. NO! HEY!

31

NO! And I can't sleep. It keeps me awake. I can't YEOW! sleep. Sometimes I go days and days without any sleep. Or all I can do is sleep sometimes, some of the time, sometimes. Ya know? Ya know? OW! Well . . . I want to live! I want to live. So I decided this was YEOW! OW! YEOW! better than that. Ya know?

Yeah

Choices. Ya know?

Yeah

Western medicine.

Western medicine, yeah.

How come you're not in school, Jesse?

I don't know.

You're a smart kid probably aren't ya?

I don't know.

Probably you're just not challenged in school.

No, I'm challenged in school. I just don't do my work.

NANCY AND MARY

Did you ever see anything like what those animals did in 206?
You have got to be some kind of beast to trash a place like that.

> **I know it. I seen a lot of messes, but I don't think I ever
> seen one as bad as that one.**

Oh, boy! it feels good to sit down.

> **It sure does.**

My corns are killing me today.

> **I got this new knee brace the doctor give me, but it don't do
> no good. And the bottoms of my feet hurt constantly. By
> mid-morning the pain is up to my knee and by quittin' time I hurt
> all the way above my hips. If I didn't have to work, I wouldn't.**

Why don't you see a doctor?

> **Oh, I seen a dozen doctors. They don't do no good.
> It's hopeless.**

Like my daughter. I don't know what she's gonna do.
I think she's afraid to get out of school. She keeps getting one
degree and then goin' back to get another. Gettin' her Ph.D. in
psychology now. Says she is going to come back and get a job
in the school system. Well, she had better make up her mind
pretty soon before she's too old to get any job at all!

> **That's right. I got a nephew like that. He don't want to work.
> All he wants to do is go to school.**

Her husband though, he's a hard worker. Got three jobs.

**Three! He sounds like the kind of man who's tried
to make a good life for his family.**

He has, but everything, you know, has been against him
from the start. I don't know how he keeps on goin',
and with that no-good, school-goin' daughter of mine too.

I guess you heard about Joline's boy's girl friend killin' herself.

I did.

**I guess she just couldn't take it no more. You know Joline and
that girl was just like mother and daughter. They never did get
married, I mean Joline's boy and that girl, but Joline and that girl
was as close as anybody ever gets. After Joline's boy got killed,
that girl just went to pieces.**

Lord.

What was that boy's name? Do you remember?

I don't think I ever knew it.

It's a wonder Joline hangs on as well she does.

I know it.

I saw Dorothy at the Diner yesterday.

You did?

MR. C. AND POETRY, TWICE

Bastards. Fucking bastards. I am a goddamned genius!
but those motherfuckers got a hermetically sealed system
and, Brother, either you play the game by their rules
or you don't get in! The bastards.

The reason my stuff never gets anywhere is because
it isn't like anybody else's. It's original, unique, one of a kind.
That's where I went wrong! I mean, I been stupid enough to think
originality counts. That's exactly what doesn't count!
Write like everybody else, you Sucker, if you want to get ahead!

Why? You ask why? Because those nitwits, those sluggardly gabbers
and tin-eared twitters can't recognize anything but what's like what
they do. And don't forget to kiss ass too. Kiss ass
and you'll get somewhere.

Sycophants. Goddamned sycophants on parade is what they are.
The bastards. Do things like everybody else does 'em and you'll
get somewhere. Follow the conventions! Do it like everybody else
does it, you asshole, and you'll get somewhere! The bastards.

Poetry's not about language! It's about something!

The only thing I've ever done is write down what I heard God say.
That was my mistake! I should have known better! Nobody cares!
Why? Why? Because God doesn't speak their withered little tongue!

They're all a bunch of disembodied, cogitarian dipshits. Ideafiers
without hands, eyes, nose, ears, lips, tongue. Pea-brained,
pure-brained, blobs of brain. A bunch of crotchless, cockless,
cuntless, thinking aparati, lexicalized cogni-buggers, ass lickers

and dingleberry pickers, decipherers and dismemberers of The Word!

Goddamn their terrible souls! Hangers on, lusters after
somebody else's life, sycophants, puss-glutted ambitionists,
tin-eared gabbers who don't know what it is to dance!
Elitist molesters of dreams, voyeuristic, life sucking, lechers
panting after visions somebody else told them to have!

You bastards, don't you know, don't you realize?

I am the Scrapple from the Apple Out of Nowhere Bird of Paradise
Trinkle Tinkle Ugly Beauty Blue Monk and Yardbird Special!

I am the very first and most original dynomotorized, 100%
organic, cockadoodledooing, altogether thoroughly Eulipion
singer of the enslaved yearners, longers, lusters, dreamers after
Freedom, Liberation, Paradise, Release!

I am the singer of the Living Destitute, The Walking Wounded.
I am The Poet of the World!

ISAIAH

Good morrow, my Children. Praise Wow. Praise Wow who giveth
and praise Wow who taketh away. Praise Wow for his creation
and for the day that he hath made.

Brothers and Sisters, open up your hearts to this poor one,
the least among you, for I am surely the servant of the Lord.
Yea, verily, I say unto you, we are all one, we are all God's
children and therefore when ye do it unto the least of these
ye do it unto me. So do it unto me, Baby!

In the beginning was the word and the word was made flesh
and the flesh dwelt among us and even though it is now later
the word is still made flesh as it is and as it always will be
in every generation for so he hath promised that verily in
every generation, Yes!, I said in every generation, for so long
as there be a run of throps, Yes! there shall be at least one of me:

the word made flesh, the avatar, incarnation of the incantations,
bagged up and bodied, right here, right now, no lines, no waiting,
and meant to dwell among you, yea, even among and, can you
believe it? in, the least of you, and therefore Brothers and Sisters!
Here I is!

Join me, join me my Brethern and Sisteren, join me so we all
can be servants of the Lord. The Lord giveth and the Lord
taketh away. I said The Lord giveth and He taketh away.
You giveth and I will taketh away! Dig deep. Dig deep, I say.
Give it up. Come on People! Give in. Give in. Give in and give!

Brothers and Sisters! Give me your money so we can all be one!
Brothers and Sisters, surely you can see that: we are one! Black

and white, rich and poor, gay and straight, old and young, Jew and Gentile, Moslem and Zoroaster!

Do you know what she said when Zorro asked her? She said, "No way, Baby. Huh, uh. Sorry, Honey!"

Come on people! You got it all and I got none. I'm tellin' you the truth, you know I am. And on top of all of that I'm givin' you a laugh too. How often you get a two-for-one sale like that? I ask you, how often? But . . . Ladies and Gentleman, you ain't payin' the bill, and that ain't right, and . . . and you know what happens to those who don't pay the bill. Ah, ah. Oh, oh. No. No. I ain't threatenin' you. I know what happens to me if I threaten you. I bat my eyes and I'm out of here, out of here and gone to where I ain't gonna need no money. No, I'm not threatening you. I'm just tellin' you the truth now. I'm out here workin' hard, workin' hard! workin' hard for you, but you ain't payin' the bill! It's time you start payin' the bill!

Prepare to meet thy maker, oh ye, sinners of Sodom and Gomorra, of Baghdad and Babylon! Thank you, sister. The Lord giveth and the Lord taketh away. You giveth and I'll taketh away. Thank you. Thank you, Brother. How's the family? Good. Good. Oh, come on now. Please! Don't be as heartless as a Republican. Black and white, rich and poor, gay and straight, old and young, Jew and Gentile, Moslem and Zoroaster--all of us are one. Give it up and give!

Praise Wow who giveth and praise Wow who taketh away. Praise Wow for his creation and for the day that he hath made. Dearly Beloved, join me now in saying as we have been taught to say and as the Apostles who came before us said:

We jeep in one Wow, Good galontly, from whom our elver amerdang. And in the ooark Bright of Wow, who was rejesten of Wow forebee elver dees and forebee elver restáning, and through whom elver amerdang came into areing, both pleezible and impleezible, rejesten ooarkly, lyon from the Good lyon, Wow of Wow, same to the Good who rejest him, nardunning to the Blamtures, whose fluration zip one zarn save lyon the Good who rejest him. And in the Wiser Gingle, whom the ooark Bright of Wow himself. Yes, our Indeed and Wow, levént to flend to the run of throps as a Daamdeedungdung, which was consupéd by the goods in ugh, but! areing unzarn to the things up oups, because the Blamtures be-bop filláin it, it seems nice that it should be zahnen by the zip spleak quilt of it in the far, and zat, samely, should the dabang fanofferly be consupéd of Good and Bright and Wiser Gingle.

Amen

Good morrow, my Children. Praise Wow. Praise Wow who giveth and praise Wow who taketh away. Praise Wow for his creation and for the day that he hath made. Brothers and Sisters, open up your hearts to this poor one, the least among you, for I am surely the servant of the Lord.

MR. RICH MAN, RICH MAN

a traditional blues

Oh, Mr. Rich Man, Rich Man
    Open up your heart and mind.
Mr. Rich Man, Rich Man
    Open up your heart and mind.
        Give the poor man a chance.
        Help stop these hard, hard times.

While you're livin' in your mansion
    You don't know what hard times mean.
Oh, you livin' in your mansion
    You don't know what hard times mean.
        Poor man's wife is starvin'
        Your wife a'livin' like a queen.

Oh, you listen to my pleadin'
    Can't stand these hard times long.
Listen to my pleadin'
    I can't stand these hard times long.
        They'll make an honest man
        do the thing that he know is wrong.

Poor man's fought all the battles.
    Poor man'll fight again today
The poor man's fought all the battles
    and he'll fight again today.
        He will do anything you ask him
            in the name of the U. S. A.

JUDY AND WAYNE: I FEEL GOOD

Okay, now, this time let's try it with you and Teddy.

Yeah.

The two of you can sit here.

Okay.

Teddy will keep you company.

Yeah.

How are you feeling, Wayne?

Good. It's okay. I feel good. I feel better.

Good.

**I feel good. It's okay. I feel good.
You can go. This is good. I feel good.**

TUESDAY I THINK

Haal comes up to Jimmy and Fred as they pass through the Park on their way home from fishing.

Hey, Haal.

Hi, Fred. Howja do?

Aw, we done okay. Nothin' to shout about.
Mostly just a lot of time to sit and think.

That's the best catch of 'em all, beats catchin' fish when you go fishin'. Catchin' fish is too much work, too hectic, too much to do. When the fishin's slow is when the fishin's good, 'cause then you can fill your bucket up with all that time to sit and think. Yeah . . . I want to go fishin' too. I ain't been fishin' in a long time. I'm going fishin' . . . next week someday. Tuesday I think. I want to go fishin' too . . . next week someday. Yessir, I'm going fishin . . . next week someday. Tuesday I think.

FRED AND NANCY

Nancy! I didn't see you sitting there.
Oh, Nancy, how have you been doing?

> **I been doin' okay.**

Fine. Fine. That is fine. I have been hoping that I would see you.
I have not seen you in a long time.

> **I know.**

I was hoping I could come around to see you. Maybe tonight.

> **No.**

I would like awfully much to see you.

> **No.**

Aw, Nancy.

> **No.**

How come you're so mean?

> **I ain't mean. I'm just mean to you!**

Aw, come on, Nancy.

> **Don't, come on, Nancy, me.**
> **I don't want to hear that kind of talk.**

Aw, Nancy. You and I could have a good time together.

Hunuh. No.

Aw, Nancy. I got nobody.

That's right! And you ain't gonna get nobody either!
At least you ain't gonna get me!

Nancy, come on, Nancy.
Why don't you just swim on over here to me.

Aw, Fred, not that fishin' line again.

Listen to me, listen to me, Nancy, please.

When I go fishin', Honey,
I go fishin' slow and deep.
I'm tellin' you the truth now. When I go fishin',
I go fishin' slow and deep.

Where's my waders?

I mean it Nancy, and
when I hook into somethin',
it ain't never somethin' I don't keep.

Listen to me, listen to me, Nancy, please,
'cause what I'm saying is: Aw, Nancy,

you just don't know
what it's like to be free
until you spend all day
in bed with me!

The hell you say! You S.O.B.
I heard about the way you do.

You ain't gonna get your hook in me!
I ain't fallin' for that fishin' line.
No sir, you ain't gonna make a fool of me. I said,
I said, you ain't never gonna make a fool of me!

I know some other fishes what been swimin' in your sea
and they done told me how you do--
you hustlin' S.O.B.
Well, you ain't never, I said never,
gonna get your hook in me.
No sir, Mr. Fisherman,
you ain't never gonna make a fool of me!

WAYNE AND JUDY:
IS THIS WHERE I'M GOING TO SLEEP TONIGHT?

Is this where I'm going to stay now? Is this where I'm going to stay?
Am I going to sleep here tonight? Where am I going to sleep tonight?
Do you know where I'm going to sleep tonight? Is this where I'm
going to stay now? Is this where I'm going to sleep tonight?

Wayne. Wayne. It's okay. I'm here.

You left me.

Wayne. It's not time to go to bed yet. It's only lunchtime.

Not hungry.

**It's okay. I'll take you back. It's okay. You've got a place to stay.
Don't you remember? You've got a room and a rocker and a TV.**

TV's broken.

**and some pictures on top of your TV. Don't you remember?
That's where you can sleep tonight: in your own bed.
And that's where you can have lunch too. Let's go back now.
Wayne, comeon. Let's go back now. I want us to go back now.**

Part Two

AIN'T IT HARD TO STUMBLE

a traditional blues

Ain't it hard to stumble
    when you got no place to fall?
Ain't it hard to stumble
    when you got no place to fall?
        Stranger here, stranger everywhere;
        I would go home, but, Honey,
            I'm a stranger there.

I'm a stranger here;
    I just blowed in your town.
I said, I'm a stranger here;
    just blowed in your town
        Just because I'm a stranger,
        everybody wants to dog me around.

Oh, I wonder how some people
    can dog a poor stranger so.
Now, I wonder how some people
    can dog a poor stranger so.
        They should remember,
        they gonna reap just what they sow.

Ain't it hard to stumble
    when you got no place to fall?
You know, it's hard to stumble
    when you got no place to fall.
        Stranger here, stranger everywhere
            You know, I would go home, but, Honey,
                I'm a stranger there.

Stranger here, stranger everywhere
You know, I would go home, but, Honey,
I'm a stranger there.

JIMMY

I come out here every day the weather's good.
I got to be around some people. Not that these days people
are all that great to be around, but somethin's better 'an nothin',
don't you think? I mean, we're a herding animal, don't you think?

I can't stand that one room, day after day, day in and day out.

It's a nice room, and I keep it nice. It's clean and I keep myself
clean too. You got to. You got to bathe, take a shower, shave
and brush your teeth, be disciplined, and you got to eat.
You got to keep yourself lookin' good even if it's not for anybody.
You can't let yourself go to pot. I'm not going to be one of those
old guys who smells like pee. That's why I get cleaned up and
put on a clean shirt and come out here every day. You got to.

It's one room and only me. You can't live that way day in, day out,
day after day. You got to be around some people.

Which is why I come out here every day,
every day the weather's good. I like people.

I didn't always live in just one room. Helen and I had a nice place,
but I got kicked out of there because they said the apartment
was too big for just one person. I got relocated. It's just a couple
blocks away from where we used to be. Relocated. Huh. Aw, it's
okay. It's big enough for me.

You come in, the bathroom's on the right, closet's on the left, then
right away, when you get into the room the kitchen's over
in the corner . . . to your right, then, you know, at the other end,
the window looks out onto the street.

It's okay. I like it. I can't complain. I got it better than alotta folks.
At least I got a roof over my head and somethin' in my belly.
That's a damn sight more than a lot of people got these days,
I'm lucky and I know it. But you can't live that way, alone all day,
day in, day out, day after day.

Aw Jesus! it gets lonely!

Nothin' to do. Nobody to talk to, nobody to be with.
I go a little crazy, you know? We weren't built to live that way.
We were meant to go two by two. We weren't meant to spend
our lives alone in just one room.

I don't even watch the damn TV. It's worse than nothing.
I just sit at the window and I watch.
On good days, I come out here.

I'd like to talk to somebody, but I don't want to force myself
on someone. I'm afraid they're gonna tell me to get lost.
All I'd like to do is talk. I get so lonely! Or maybe we could
go over to the Diner and get a coffee, you know, sit in there
and talk. But I'm afraid I'll get rejected.

Well, I'm out here now. At least that's somethin'. Maybe someday
I'll get up my courage and I'll say something to someone.
I got my hope, my hope for that. At least that's somethin'.

Like I said, I'm lucky and I know it, but . . .
Jesus! It gets lonely!

MISS FORTY

You from around here? Where you from?

I'm not from around here either. I'm from down near Belly-fon-tane.
People think it's Bellefountain--the beautiful fountain--but
those of us from down that way know its just plain old
Belly-fon-tane. Where you from?

Chillicothe? Athens? Akron? Fort Defiance?
You from McConnelsville, Beverly? How about Mingo Junction?
Now there's one for ya! Mingo Junction. I knew a guy from there once.
I knew a guy once from there. . . . Both of those.
It was the same guy.

Where you from? Akron, Canton, Toledo? I bet it's Westerville or
Worthington or Waverly or West Carrolton. You from Cincinnati?
I know you ain't from Cleveland. Nobody with hair and a shirt
like yours is ever from Cleveland.

Me? I'm from Ashtabula. Right next door to Conneaut. No. Really.
I am. Born and bred . . . well . . . in Ashtabula. Yes sirree.

   Samovar and Zeemahoolah
   Lived in a house in Ashtabula.
   Ashtabula, O-hi-o.
   That's the place we want to go!

Christ, I bet you know that one. You know that one, don't ja?
It's a kids book, well, a novel. Oh, it's so sad.

Me? I'm from Ashtabula. Ashtabula, O-hi-o.

Here! look at this map. See? Ashtabula, O-hi-o.
Right there on the lake. Isn't it beautiful?
Oh, it's lovely right there on the lake.

But I ain't goin' back there or anywhere is my guess.
I'm stuck here is what I think. They won't let me go nowhere.
I'm here to stay is what I think.

Oh, God, I sure would like to get away, get out and see some
places. I'd like to go to Cincinnati and take a ride on one of them
river boats, you know, the ones with the paddle wheels. What
they call them kind of boats? Paddlewheelers. Yeah, that's it. I'd
like to go see Columbus. See the Capital. Hell, I never even been to
Akron. I never been anywhere, except Ashtabula . . . and here. . . .

They got me here to stay. Forty years old and here to stay.
Forty years old. Can you believe that? I know, I know, I don't look it,
but I am. Forty years old and I ain't never been to Akron.
I ain't ever even been to Steubenville! But I read my maps.
You bet I do. Got one right here. Wanna see?

Forty years old and never been anywhere. Well, hey!
life begins at forty, right? Ain't that what they say? Hell,
I got time. Right? That's what they say, ain't it? I mean,
I'm still just a kid. Right?

Just another couple seconds, please! Really. Please!

Oh, God! how I would like to get away . . .
just for a little while, but I know I never will.
I never will. Forty years old and here to stay. . . .

Well! it's been nice talking with you. See, I told you it'd only be
a couple more seconds. You got a nice shirt. I gotta go. Got to run.

56

Got a lot of things I got to do today.

Oh, hell! it ain't true. I know you know it ain't.
I got nothin' to do. Not a damn thing. I never do.

Say, I like you. What say . . . what say you and me--what say
you and me--we go over to the Diner and get a coffee. Wadaya say?
Just the two of us, you and me, we'll go over to the Diner
and we'll get a coffee.

Hey! wait a minute! Let's go over to the Diner. Come on.
Hey! Where you goin'?

LET'S TRY IT AGAIN

Let's try it again.

Okay.

I think it'll be okay this time.

Okay.

Okay.

Good.

Good.

**I feel good. It's okay. I feel good.
You can go. This is good. I feel good.**

Good.

Good.

Okay. Bye.

Okay Bye.

JESSE, KATHY, AND SHAUN, AGAIN

What I'd like most is: I'd like to quit school.

**God, no, Jesse. You'd better not. I mean . . .
Don't do it. Don't quit school. Really.**

Kathy, you said our rule was nobody could tell anybody
anything about what to do. We all just get to say
what we want.

Oh, yeah. Okay. I forgot. Okay. Sorry, Jesse.

How about you Kathy.

**What would I like most? What I'd like more than anything is
to go home and take a bath, with lots of hot water . . . and soap
that smells good and bubble bath . . . and a back brush . . . and
a radio. I'd stay in there so long my fingers and my toes
would shrivel up. And a thick bath mat . . . and soft towels
. . . and some sweet smelling talcum powder . . . and a
heavy terry cloth robe . . .and . . . some fuzzy slippers and . . .
Oh! . . . yeah.**

Shaun.

I'd like to sit here quietly all day.

HAAL'S GREAT IDEA

Mr. C. Ah, Mr. C. You . . .You, ah, got a minute?
I know you're busy and all but . . .

What is it, Haal? I'm busy.

I know. I know. But . . . I . . . well, I'm sick of doin' bottles.
I want to expand, advance, and I got this idea how I could
pull myself up by my own shoestrings.

Good idea, kid.

That's right. I . . . I want to go into business . . . for myself I mean.
I want to make . . . T-shirts. I mean, I seen how many people
go around in T-shirts what say something, and I got that idea.
I thought I could go into the business, I mean, that is, if
somebody could get me started . . . you know, put up some
money . . . to get me started.

Good idea, Kid! Go for it!

I went ahead and worked out my idea. I mean without any help
from you or anybody, and I was wondering if I could show it to
you.

Okay, Haal, but only just a minute. I'm busy.

Great. You're gonna love this one, Mr. C. Oh, this one is so good.
It's my T-shirts idea. I printed up a few and . . . here it is!

*Haal takes out of a plastic bag a T-shirt
on the front of which it says:*

LIFE HURTS

**God! Nobody wants that, Haal! Nobody wants to hear about
or think about that pain and suffering thing. Take it from me,
there's no money in the suffering game, Haal.**

Is that so?

**Yeah, that's so. And besides, that phrase, LIFE HURTS,
it's worse than poetry. That T-shirt is ridiculous!
You are such a simpleton!**

Well then, how about: GROWING OLD IS NOT FOR SISSIES.

Oh, that's another good one. That'll sell real well.

Yeah, and I got another one too: SOME PEOPLE ARE
SARCASTIC AND MEAN. Holy Cow, Mr. C., just because you're
a poet and know all them big words don't mean you're
better'n me. And besides, so what if I am simple. It's a
gift to be simple. You're mean Mr. C. You hurt my feelings.
But I know you don't care. Maybe I am simple. So What!
You. . . you should try it. You should try it out sometime,
you . . . you . . . dirty rotten stinker, you . . . poophead!

**Aw, Jeeze! Haal. Haal. Wait a minute, Haal.
I didn't mean . . . . All I meant was it's about as dumb
as poetry. Haal! Hey, wait a minute. What I meant was:
it's like poetry. It is poetry. Nobody wants it. People don't care.**

I think they do.

I don't.

And I think I'm gonna make it too.

I thought that once.

How come you're so down all the time?

That's a good question. I don't like good questions.

So how come you're so down all the time?

I just told you.

Because you never made it?

Yeah.

Well, maybe if you didn't feel so sorry for yourself all the time, you wouldn't be so blue. Anyway, it's gonna be different for me.

Maybe so, kid. Maybe so.

What I was thinkin' was we pass out samples, see?

We?

Yeah.

Us?

Yeah.

So, this is the way it ends for me. Stuck here, abandoned in this backwater for the refuse of the world, and me, right here with all the rest of these miscreants and cripples.

What?

Nothing.

What's mis-crints?

**Nothing. Now I understand how Ma felt
when I put her in the nursing home.**

What?

Nothing!

So, you in on this with me?

What?

Passin' out samples and stuff. My T-shirts idea.

**Aw, hell, why not? What the hell.
It's no more ridiculous than my poetry.**

You said it. Not me.

We're both just small time entrepreneurs.

That's right, small time engineers. Just the two of us.

Hell, at least I'm still out here, right?

Right.

**At least I'm still peddlin' poems. At least I haven't given up.
At least I still got a career to be disappointed in!**

That's right. You got to have something to be disappointed in.

**Yeah, at least I'm still peddlin' poems.
At least I'm not workin' in a friggin' bank!**

That's right! We'll give 'em to the regulars around here.

Do what?

The T-shirts, the samples.

Huh?

That way each of them's like a walkin'
advertisement for us, ya know?

Who?

The regulars . . . around here.
That's the way to do it. That way
we build up our business, ya know?

Yeah, I know. I know.

And when my LIFE HURTS T-shirt gets goin', then I'm gonna
bring out the GROWING OLD IS NOT FOR SISSIES one.

Ma woulda liked that one.

So let's go get 'em. Okay?

Okay.

I got 'em down to my place,
under my bed. So let's go.

To your place?

Yeah.

Your place?

Yeah.

You wanna go get 'em yourself?

Ah . . . yeah.

FRED AND JUDY: LET'S TALK

Let's talk.

What?

Let's talk. I need somebody to talk to. Let's talk.

I don't know you.

Not yet. Of course you don't. Not yet. But after I begin to talk, then you'll begin to get to know me.

Wait! How can you get to know me if you leave?

Did it ever occur to you that I might not want to know you?

Why?

Why?

Why.

You have got some kind of nerve. Why? Because I already know too many people as it is. I already have to relate to too many people already. Why do you think I was out here in the park trying to read my book in the first place--anyway? I was out here in the Park to get away from all those people I know, all those people I have to relate to all the time. I want to be alone with my book and my thoughts. I want to be alone. Alone. I don't want to relate to you or to the people at work or my clients or my partner or my kids. I want to be alone! Which means: I don't want to know you.

But I'm lonely.

So what! I don't care! I'm lonely too.
I got everybody in the world wanting to talk to me
and I'm lonely too.

You mean, everybody in the world wants to talk to you,
wants you to listen, but nobody wants you to talk to them,
nobody wants to listen to you.

That's right, and I'm sick of it.

I bet you are.

I am. I have had it. All I do is listen! I am sick of it. Years ago,
when I was younger and just starting out, oh, oh, I took such
pride in how I could listen. You just don't know.
I mean, I could listen!

I bet.

I got a rush out of it. It was such a high. I mean, sexual even.
It was like . . . well . . . Oh, god, how I could listen, and the
more I listened the more people admired me, looked up to me,
loved me. I was so good at it. It was a rush. I got off on it, and
. . . well . . . what else is there? what else could I ask for?

Not much.

Then, suddenly, one day. No. It was slowly. Slowly, I realized
that I was only listening so that people would love me. I realized
I was dependent on people talking to me and my listening
to them and them falling in love with me and getting all hot
for me because I was such a good listener and cared so much
for them and was so selfless and intent on them instead of all of
that for me. Slowly, I realized that I did all this listening so that
people would think I was perfect and also so that I could hide

myself from everybody. I mean, if you are always listening to others and giving yourself to others, and being nice to others and good to others, other people never have a chance to get to know you.

I know.

It was the perfect defense against ever revealing myself to anyone. What I did made me appear to be the ultimately humble person, oh, so selfless and giving. What a crock. And all the while it was a cover for my ultimate vanity and my absolute desire to conceal myself from everyone. I just kept the focus on them all the time and they never had a chance to find out anything about me.

Not anymore!

Slowly, I realized I was doing all this listening to protect myself, keep myself . . . hidden.

You've said that.

I am aware of that!
I'm sorry. I apologize.

No need to.

My whole life was dedicated to being hidden
while doing all those things people would love me for.

Oh, dear, that's not very good grammar.

It's good enough.

Yes. It is. It really doesn't matter if you end a sentence with a preposition, does it?

Not anymore.

> That's right. Not anymore it doesn't.
> And I'll say ain't too, if I feel like it.

Good for you!

> And I'm not going to say *an historical* anymore either!

Let it all hang out!

> Don't you get fresh with me!

I'm not.

> I think you are.
> You just keep those lewd and lascivious comments to yourself!

What?

> You know what I'm talking about.

I don't.

> You said, let it all hang out.

I didn't mean that by that.

> I know what you meant. Don't tell me what you meant.
> I'm in the business. You park loonies are all alike.
> You're all sexual perverts, I know that.
> I know what you meant.

I am not loony. I am lonely.

Well, at least you have a little linguistic wit.

Have what?

At least you're interested in words. Playing with words. You're sensitive to the sounds of words.

I am?

Yes. You are.

Oh.

What?

I just said, Oh.

Why?

I don't know why.

Are you being sarcastic?

Of course not.

Then you must have trouble hearing.

What?

You're a comedian, aren't you?

No.

You're trying out routines on me, aren't you?

What?

You do have trouble hearing, don't you?

No. I have trouble understanding.

Where was I?

Where you were.

What?

You were where you are.

What are you talking about?

Did you leave?

No.

Then you are where you were
and you were where you are.

What?

Right here! Right here!

What are you talking about!

It looks to me, ma'am . . . it seems to me . . .
and I know I could be mistaken, but
in this particular instance, I believe I am not . . .
mistaken, that is, because . . . it looks to me, ma'am,

as if you are in just about exactly the same place you were.

Oh, no! I mean verbally, not physically.

Verbally.

I didn't leave.

I didn't think you did.

Verbally.

Ah, yes, verbally.

Where was I?

Where you were.

But where was that?

Verbally?

Yes!

Ah!

I was talking about something.

You said I was something.

Don't flatter yourself.

What?

Nothing. What was I talking about?

You said I was something.

I did?

Yes.

**Oh, yes. I said you were, you are,
sensitive to the sounds of words.**

I am?

Yes. You said, "I am not loony, I am lonely."

That's sensitive?

**Yes. Loony. Lonely. The near rhyme. The subtle similarity in
sound yet also the difference between the diphthong oo in loony
and the long o in lonely. oo/o. And the same subtle similarity
yet difference between the long e sound in loony and the ly
in lonely. ee/ly.**

Oh.

Are you making fun of me?

Of course not.

I think you are. You're being sarcastic.

I?

You see? That proves it.

It does?

You're no park loony, are you?

I told you I wasn't.

You're a professor or a writer or something, right?

Right.

Right what?

What?

Which?

Which what?

Oh for god's sake! Yes! You're a professor or a writer or something. Is that not correct?

Right.

Right which?

Right or something.

Why do you have to be so sarcastic all the time?

It's not sarcasm. It's what you call my "linguistic wit."

You've been listening to me?

Sure.

Then why did you make me change the subject?

What subject?

You know very well what subject.

I do?

Don't get cute with me. Yes. You do.

Oh.

I don't want to talk about grammar.

I thought we were talking about sexual perversion.

You see? I was right. You are trying to manipulate me.

I am?

You certainly are.
You are trying to force me to attend to your agenda.

I am not.

You are.
I don't want to talk about grammar!

I don't either!

Good.

Who would?

Exactly. Who would?
I want to talk about what I was talking about.

What was that?

About me and how I never get to talk because I've always got to
listen and how I am fed up with that, fed up to the gills,
to the top of my gills with that, up to the brim
and even above the brim.

That's a mixed metaphor.

There you go again. I said I didn't want to talk about grammar.

Sorry.

Besides, it isn't.

It isn't what?

A mixed metaphor. It is two separate metaphors,
one following the other but each separate from the other.
The metaphors are independent and sequential.
They are not mixed.

Sorry.

You've done it again. Stop it.

What?

And stop that too!

Bossy, ain't ya?

You know what.

I do?

Yes, you do.

Yes, well, you did it this time.

Did what?

Started talking about grammar.

I did not.

You most certainly did.

I didn't!

You did!

Well . . . maybe I did.

Your first concession.

In any event I'm sick of it.

Grammar?

**No! You know very well what I am talking about.
I am talking about what I've been talking about all along.**

About not being able to talk.

Yes!

Go for it!

I will.

Good.

I'm sick of it.

You are sick of never being able to talk.

**Yes! How come nobody ever listens to me!
I've got things to say too you know.**

Yes, I know!

How would you know? You don't even know me.

I'm getting to.

Getting to what?

Getting to know you.

**Oh, no. No you don't! I don't want to play guessing games
either. I have told you I am not going to attend to your agenda,
no matter what it is.
And I am also going to keep you on the subject.**

Good.

Only don't think I don't know the answer.

The answer?

It's *South Pacific*.

What?

That song is from *South Pacific*.

What song?

"Getting To Know You."

The King and I.

What?

"Getting to Know You" is from *The King and I*.

It is?

Yes.

Damn!

Sorry.

I don't want to play trivial guessing games.

I don't either.

Good.

Who would?

Exactly, who would?

Exactly.

I want to talk about what I was talking about.

And what was that?

Ah! You said you didn't want to do that.

True. Okay. Go ahead

**I want to talk about me and how I never get to talk because
I've always got to listen and how I am fed up with that
and don't you think I am going to be foolish enough
to put a metaphor in here this time
and give you the chance to divert me again.
I'm not going to give you that chance a second time.**

What chance?

You said you didn't want to do that!

Okay. Okay.

**I am so sick of not being able to talk. I want to talk
and be listened to, I mean, really listened to.
Do you know what I mean?**

Oh, yes ma'am, I do!

**I mean really listened to, cared for and listened to.
I need somebody to talk to who will just listen, take it in
and hold it there and not judge it or grade it or argue with it
but just take it in and accept it and hold it and be quiet about it,
maybe have a little fun with it, but not judge it.**

Yes.

Like . . . like you've been doing.

I?

Yes.

I have?

Yes.
Could we talk?

No.

Why not?

Because I'm lonely and I need someone to talk to.

You could talk to me.

I haven't been able to yet.

But I don't know you.

How could you? You've been doing all the talking.

Please. I'm lonely. I need someone to talk to.

So do I.

We could talk to each other.

No.

Why not?

Because you don't know me.

> **Of course I don't. Not yet. But after you begin to talk then I'll begin to get to know you.**

That's my line.

> **You don't own it.**

True.

> **Okay, so, you begin to talk and after a little while I'll begin to get to know you.**

No.

> **Why not?**

Because you said you didn't want to know me.

> **I've changed my mind.**

I doubt it.

> **Wait. Please.**
> **How . . . How can I get to know you if you leave?**

When I said that to you, you said, "I don't want to know you."

> **You've been listening to me.**

Yes.

> **Did I really say I didn't want to know you?**

Yes.

And it hurt you.

Yes.

I'm sorry.

Well . . .

I'm sorry.

It happens all the time.

**I know it does.
I've done all the talking.**

Yes.

You could have a turn.

No.

I thought you said you wanted to talk.

I did.

Go ahead.

I've changed my mind.

Why?

Because it doesn't do any good! What good does it do?

I don't think any.

We just get confused.

Yes.

So we talk some more.

Yes.

And we hide.

Yes.

Whether we listen or we talk.

Yes.

It doesn't do any good!

No.

May I touch you?

What?

I want to touch you.

Where?

Wherever I may.

I don't think so.

I want to.

I'm afraid.

So am I.
May I put my arm around you?

No.

May I hold your hand?

No.

What then? Something.

**You may sit close enough to me
so that our shoulders are touching.**

And our thighs.

Certainly not.

Our knees.

Well . . . we'll see . . . . Maybe later.

Thank you.

This is nice.

Yes.

**You'd better go. I mean, I'd better go.
I'm late. Good-bye. Thank you.**

NANCY AND JUDY AGAIN

I got off early.

> **I got off early.**

Who was that?

> **I don't know. Some guy who sat down next to me. . .**
> **I was out here reading, he came along, he sat down next to me.**

You were rubbing up against him.

> **We were touching shoulders.**

Touching shoulders?

> **Yeah.**

What is that?

> **I don't know!**

Do you know his name?

> **No.**

That's Fred.

> **Who?**

Fred.

> **You know him?**

No matter what you say, Nancy. No matter what you need.

What are you talking about?

No matter where you are, Nancy, you can count on me.
Why did you do that?

Do what?

Come on to him like that.

**I didn't! I was out here reading, he came along,
he sat down next to me. We talked.**

I saw you!

So what!

Love at first sight.

No!

It was.

No. I don't know. He was nice.

Just like that.

No!

Are you going to see him again?

I don't even know his name.

You're lying.

I'm not!

You are!

I'm not! What do you want me to say! I won't see him again. There. Are you happy?

But you want to see him again!

Oh, for Christ's sake. Let's forget this!

Easier said than done.

I'm sorry. Nothing happened. What's wrong with you! I don't want to fight.

You never want to fight! You never want to fight with me!

I don't like fighting!

Well, I do!

HAAL AND T-SHIRTS

*Haal and Mr. C both appear
with armloads of T-shirts.*

Hey, everybody,
wait'll you see what I got.
I got my new T-shirts idea.
I'm gonna make a bundle.
Here. Take one. They're free samples.
It's my advertising.
I'm gonna make a bundle.
And Mr. C. here's gonna help me out too,
aren't you Mr. C.

Yes, Haal. I'm going to help you out.

THE PURSE LADY AND MR. C. AGAIN

So since when did you decide to be one of the people?

What are you talkin' about?

I'm talkin' about what a hypocrite you are, and what a whiner
you are too. You're such a baby. You got no guts.

Oh yeah?

Yeah. Piss and moan is all you ever do, complainin' all the time
about how you're stuck here in "this dump, this backwater
with all the rest of these miscreants and cripples."

Like you!

Like you! You ain't exactly every teenaged maiden's
vision of sweet poetic ephemerality.

Sweet poetic ephemerality?

Yeah. Back off Mr. Poet Man, you ain't the only one knows how to talk.
And don't try to change the subject. We're talkin' about
what a hypocrite and whiner you are.

I ain't talkin' about it!

Well, I am. I'm talkin' about you're just like all the rest the poets.
You talk up a storm with that vocabulary, but you don't never
mean nothing you say.

Oh, yeah?

Yeah. It's all just words to you. You spin a tale
full of sound and fury but you don't signify nuthin'.

I could signify on you!

For example, you got a job. And you got that inheritance
from your mother too. What kind of poet are you
with money comin' in every week?

Get out of here.

You're no poet. You're a fake poet. Poets don't have money comin'
in from their poor dead mothers--God rest her soul--every week.

What are you talkin' about?

I'm talkin' about you got a nest egg.

Oh, yeah. A pullet egg.

Why, you're even worse than I thought you were. You're
ungrateful too. You shouldn't talk that way about your
poor dead mother, God rest her soul.

Don't tell me how I should talk about Ma.

Your mother. Didn't your mother ever tell you:
Don't look a gift horse in the mouth?

Ma never told me about you!

You ought to be ashamed of yourself talking that way
about your poor dead mother--God rest her soul.

Too bad I can't say the same for you.

And those poems you write; they're terrible poems.

Like you know about poetry.

I know about poetry plenty, and I knew your mother too
and I don't think she'd like the way you write.

Oh, yeah?

Yeah. Those poems you write, the way you talk in them,
it's filthy. You call that poetry?

Yeah, I call that poetry.

Elizabeth Barrett Browning is poetry.

Ah, jeeze!

What do you know from poetry?

More than you know from nothing!

Your mother, she didn't trust you.

You never knew my mother!

She thought you were retarded with all that poetry you write.
She knew you'd never amount to nothing. That's why she gave
her Japanese garden to the city for a park so you could have a job,
so the poor, retarded poet-boy could have a job.

Fer Christ's sake! I keep tellin' you, you never knew Ma.

You're a foul-mouthed, nasty-person too.

Thank you very much.

I think you should do something for these people.

I do!

You don't do nothing! All you do is sit around all day and write that filthy poetry.

Screw you!

See? Your mother, she would be rolling over in her grave if she could hear the way you are talking to me.

Roll over, Ma!

Oh, the way you talk about your poor dead mother--God rest her soul.

I'm out here ain't I? I'm out here with my thumb in the dike, ain't I? I'm out here lookin' after this place and all you miscreants and cripples, ain't I? That's not something?

Your poetry is just obscenities. It's not poetry.

I'm out here holding back the chaos all around us, ain't I?

It's not nice. It's not nice the way you talk.

You think it's easy holdin' down this fort?
At least because of me you bunch of weirdos got a place to be.

What are you saying?

I'm saying you should be grateful.

You're telling me what I should be grateful for?

You're goddamned right.

You should be grateful your mother can't hear the way you talk.

You should be grateful Ma is dead.

Oh, my god, the way you talk.

REPRISE

So am I gonna see you at the Diner tomorrow?

Aw, I don't know.

The special's gonna be Shepherd's Pie.

I like Shepherd's Pie.

So, am I gonna see you?

• • • • •

Haal, I been thinkin' . . . about our T-shirts business.

Yeah?

I think our next one, I mean the one after GROWING OLD IS NOT FOR SISSIES should be IT'S A GIFT TO BE SIMPLE.

That's a good one.

• • • • •

Tomorrow, Wayne, tomorrow how about you sit out here without your Teddy Bear.

I don't think so.

You could just try it.

I don't think so.

Or maybe you could let me use Teddy
tomorrow. How about that? I think
I need him worse than you do.

I don't think so.

• • • • •

I'd like to come home . . .
just for a little while . . .

You can't.

Just for an hour.

No, I don't trust you.

Just to talk.

It's too late.

• • • • •

Awright, people, everybody out.
The denizens of the night returneth.
Time for you to go. Come on, now.
It's not safe here after dark.

You should put lights.

Yeah, yeah, I know.
We'll talk about it tomorrow.

THE END

AN AFTERWORD

This book is raw material that could be a play, with or without music, an opera, presented in a theatre, or outside at noon every day in a park, or in a church, or . . . or . . . or . . . In short, I hope theatre companies will use this book as a text to mount a production of PARK SONGS, all of it or parts of it. The choice is yours.

There could also be a little blues band that acts as a Greek chorus reacting to what is happening in the Park, predicting what will happen. I can make suggestions for tunes, songs, the band could play that I think are appropriate to the various scenes. Or the band can come up with its own music.

Some scenes here like "Let's Talk" are short, one-act plays unto themselves and can be played that way. I've always imagined someone doing "Let's Talk" three times in a single evening, once with a man and a woman, once with two women and once with two men. The text would stay the same for all three plays only the casting would change.

Or you could select out the scenes with the same characters, such as the scenes with Judy and Wayne or Jimmy and Miss Forty, or all the scenes with Mr. C. and Purse Lady, maybe adding Haal. In the last scene between Mr. C. and Purse Lady, Haal could be there and react to what is going on but say nothing.

Or you could do a combination of scenes making up a cohesive play of any length you want. As I said before, the choice is yours. These are, obviously, only suggestions. The possibilities for combinations of scenes, various arrangements, venues, locations are limited only by the imaginations of those who produce a particular show. Have at it.

For permission to mount a production contact the publisher, Exterminating Angel Press, c/o Tod Davies, 1892 Colestin Road, Ashland, OR 97520 USA, or write to Tod at: info@exterminatingangel.com

David Budbill

ACKNOWLEDGEMENTS

"Mr Rich Man, Rich Man" *Exterminating Angel Press*, September 2011

"Mr. C and Poetry, Once" *Exterminating Angel Press*, July 2011

"Wayne" *Exterminating Angel Press*, November 2009

"Nancy and Kathy" "Judy and Nancy" *Exterminating Angel Press*, February 2008

"Jimmy" *Exterminating Angel Press*, January 2008

"Miss Forty" "Jeanie" "Purse Lady" appeared in revised versions in *Exterminating Angel Press*, December 2007

"Miss Forty" "Wayne" "Jimmy" *Entelechy International*, Number 3, 2005

"Purse Lady" *Saranac Review*, Vol I, No. 1, Fall 2005

"Jimmy" "Miss Forty" *Graffiti* Rag, #3, 1997-1998

"Jeanie" *For A Living: The Poetry of Work*, edited by Nicholas Coles and Peter Oresick, University of Illinois Press, 1995, Isbn: 0-252-06410-0

"The Mad Poet, Twice" *Dog Pond Review*, Fall 1989

"I'm Worried" *The Ohio Review*, #44, 1989

"Mr Rich Man, Rich Man" and "Ain't It Hard to Stumble" are traditional blues discovered by Odetta on a recording at The Smithsonian Institution, probably made early in the 20th century. I transcribed the lyrics from an Odetta recording of unknown origins.

DAVID BUDBILL was born in Cleveland, Ohio and has worked as a carpenter's apprentice, short order cook, Christmas tree farm day laborer, mental hospital attendant, church pastor, teacher, and occasional commentator on NPR's *All Thing Considered*. He is also the award-winning author of twelve books of poems, six plays, a novel, a collection of short stories, an opera libretto, and a picture book for children. His books include the bestselling *Happy Life* (Copper Canyon, 2011) and *Judevine*, a collection of narrative poems that forms the basis for *Judevine: The Play*, which has been performed in twenty-two states. He lives in the mountains of northern Vermont, where he tends his garden.

R. C. IRWIN, whose absurdist and nostalgic work provides the set design for *Park Songs*, is a native San Franciscan. He teaches at San Francisco City College.